THE BIG BOOK OF
ACTIVITIES

Peg Connery-Boyd

Illustrations by Scott Waddell

Published by Sourcebooks Jabberwocky, an imprint of Sourcebooks, Inc.
P.O. Box 4410, Naperville, Illinois 60567-4410
(630) 961-3900
Fax: (630) 961-2168
www.sourcebooks.com

Source of production: Versa Press, East Peoria, Illinois, USA
Date of production: February 2016
Run number: 5005854

Printed and bound in the United States of America.
VP 10 9 8 7 6 5 4 3 2

HI, *Kansas City* **Royals** FAN!

RETIRED HEROES

Unscramble the names of the *Royals* heroes
on the jerseys below.

HOWSER

_____

_____

Solution is on page 49.

FOLLOW THE BALL
Which pitcher threw the strike?

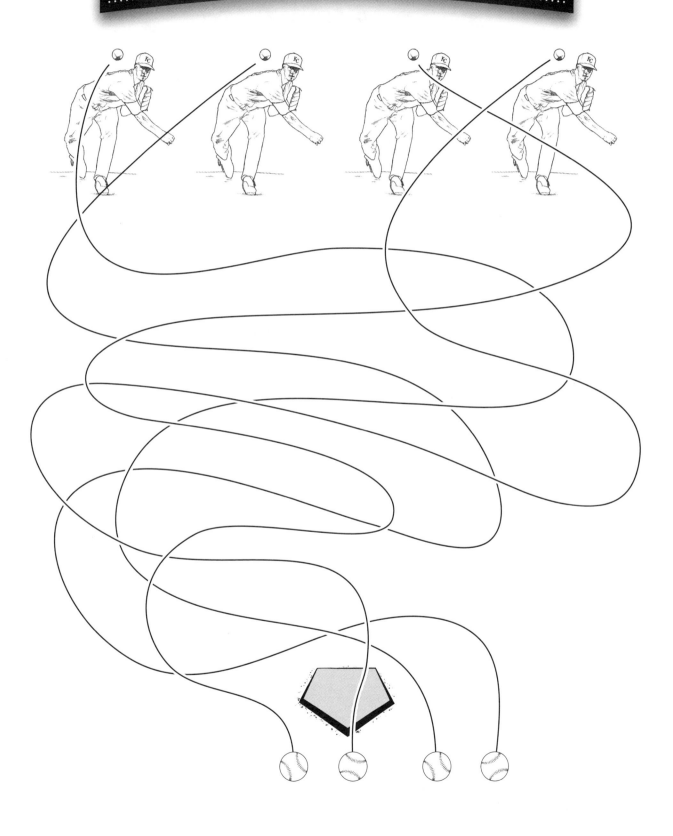

Solution is on page 49.

3

CONNECT THE DOTS

HINT!
A true *Royals* fan never leaves home without it!

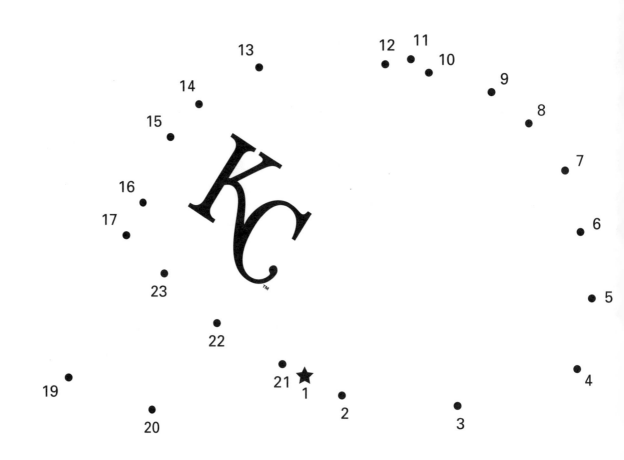

13

12 11 10

14

15   9

8

7

16

17   6

18   5

23

22   4

21 ★
19   1
20   2   3

4

FIND THE DIFFERENCES

Can you find all **three** differences between the two images below?

Solution is on page 50.

START HERE

Solution is on page 50.

WHICH IMAGE IS DIFFERENT?

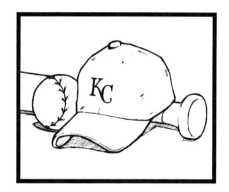

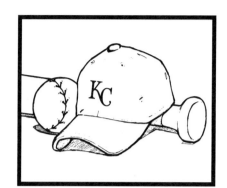

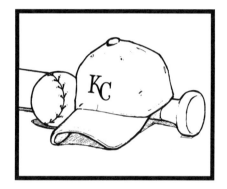
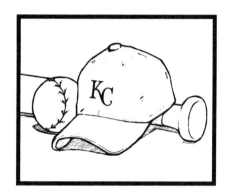

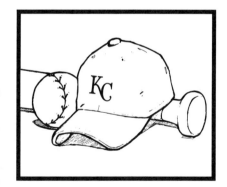

Solution is on page 51.

LET'S DRAW!

Use the grid to draw the *Royals* logo.

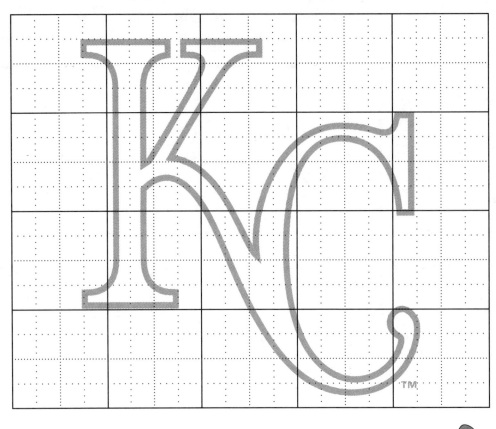

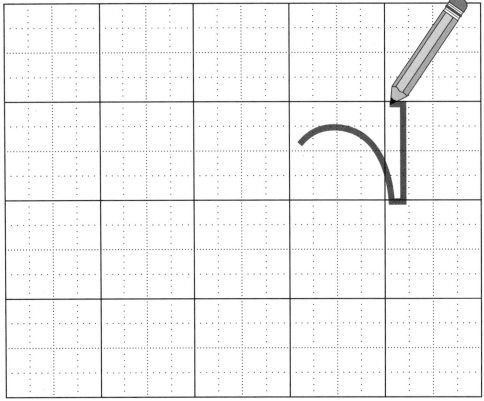

____ ____ ____ ____ ____ ____ _E__

____ ____ ____ ____ ____

KEY

= A	= F	= O	= V
= E	= L	= R	= Y

Solution is on page 51.

9

LABEL THE PARTS OF A BASEBALL FIELD

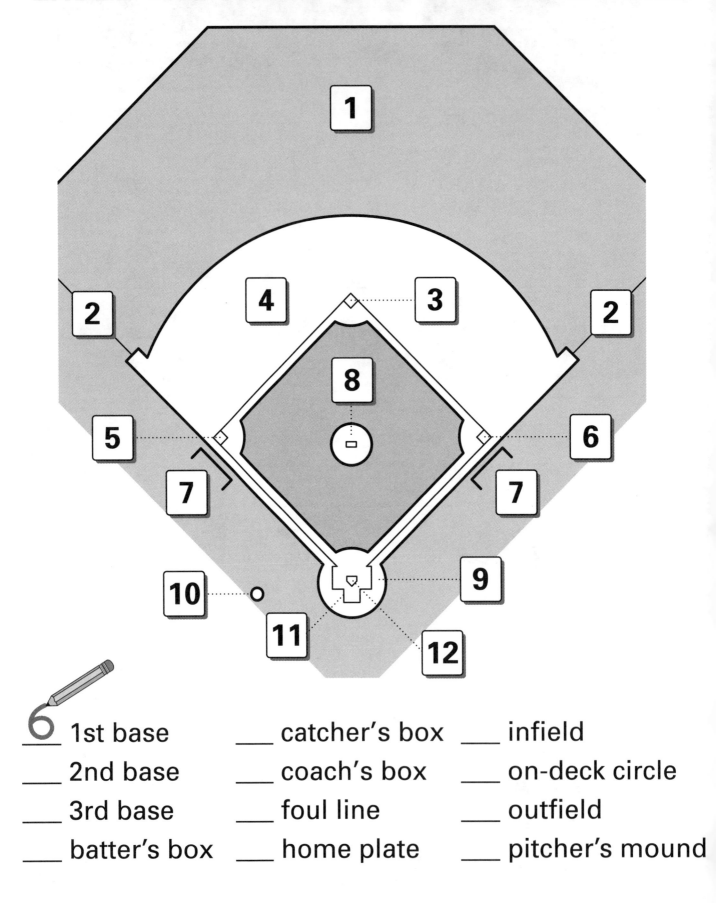

___ 1st base   ___ catcher's box   ___ infield

___ 2nd base   ___ coach's box   ___ on-deck circle

___ 3rd base   ___ foul line   ___ outfield

___ batter's box   ___ home plate   ___ pitcher's mound

Solution is on page 52.

SCRAMBLE

Unscramble the letters of these *Kauffman Stadium*™ snacks.

DOAS

SODA

OTH GDO

___ ___ ___   ___ ___ ___

ROCPOPN

___ ___ ___ ___ ___ ___ ___

ZEPRTEL

___ ___ ___ ___ ___ ___ ___

CIE MCEAR

___ ___ ___   ___ ___ ___ ___ ___

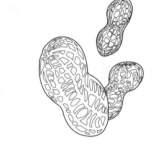

NUPTEAS

___ ___ ___ ___ ___ ___ ___

Solution is on page 52.

CONNECT THE DOTS

35
36
34
25
26
24
15
16
14
5
6
4
37
33
27
23
17
13
7
3
38
32
28
22
18
12
8
2
31
29
21
19
11
9
30
20
10

★1

39
40

46

45
41

44
42

43

KAUFFMAN STADIUM™

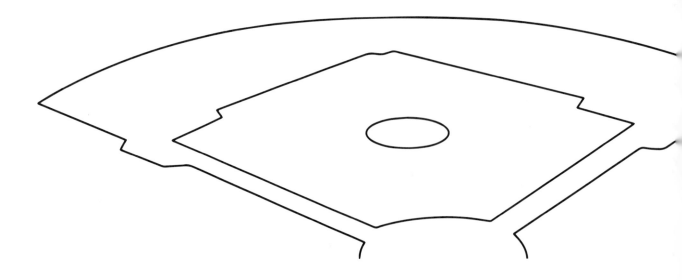

WORD SEARCH

```
T P T M C H O F R J L
W W H I T E X U F K L
B U A S B O W Y O A M
J K N S L L C E U N F
C R A O F O U N N S G
V O R U P I N E T A R
Y M S R F K T E A S O
B Y S I D F F Z I C Y
A P L J V E M S N I A
E G K P R J O A S T L
D A M E R I C A N Y S
```

AMERICAN	KANSAS CITY	PINE TAR
BLUE	KAUFFMAN	ROYALS
FOUNTAINS	MISSOURI	WHITE

Solution is on page 53.

BATTER UP!

CROSSWORD PUZZLE

Use your knowledge of baseball to solve the puzzle.

Across

1. The pitcher stands on the pitcher's _____ when he throws the baseball.
5. After the batter hits the ball, he runs toward _____ base.
6. The player who throws the ball toward home plate for the batter to hit is called the _____.
9. To score a run, the player must touch _____ plate.

Down

2. The _____ calls the balls and strikes.
3. Each baseball player wears a baseball _____ on his head.
4. Three strikes and you're _____!
7. The player who crouches behind home plate is called the _____.
8. A baseball player wears a _____ on his hand to catch the ball.

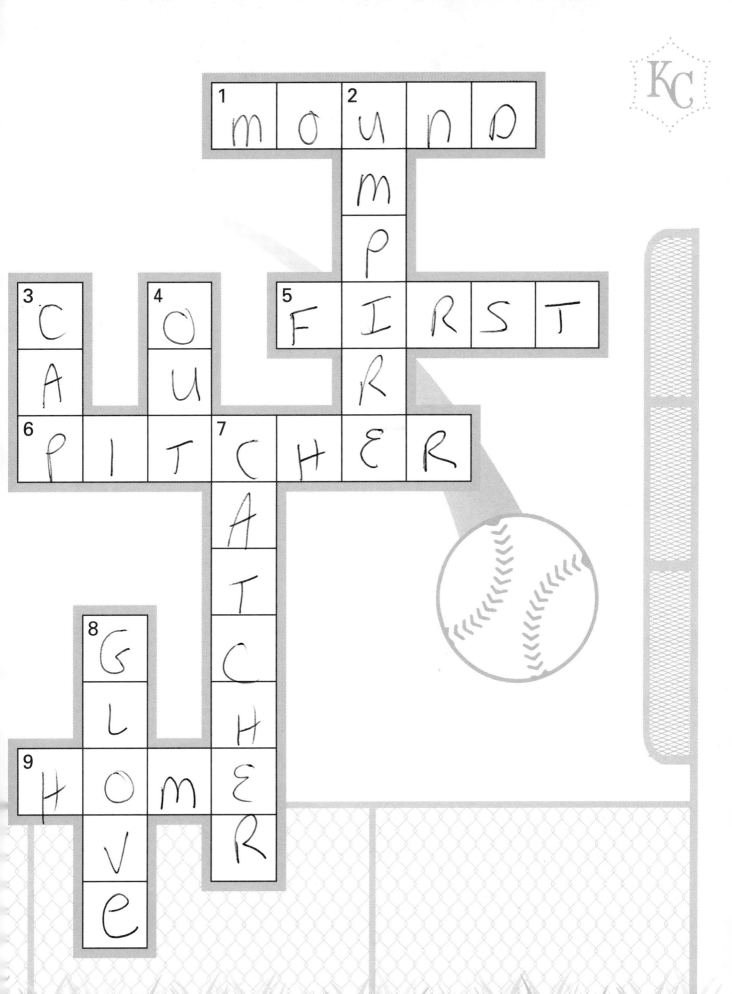

Across

1. MOUND
5. FIRST
6. PITCHER
9. HOME

Down

2. UMPIRE
3. CAP
4. OUT
7. CATCHER
8. GLOVE

CONNECT THE DOTS

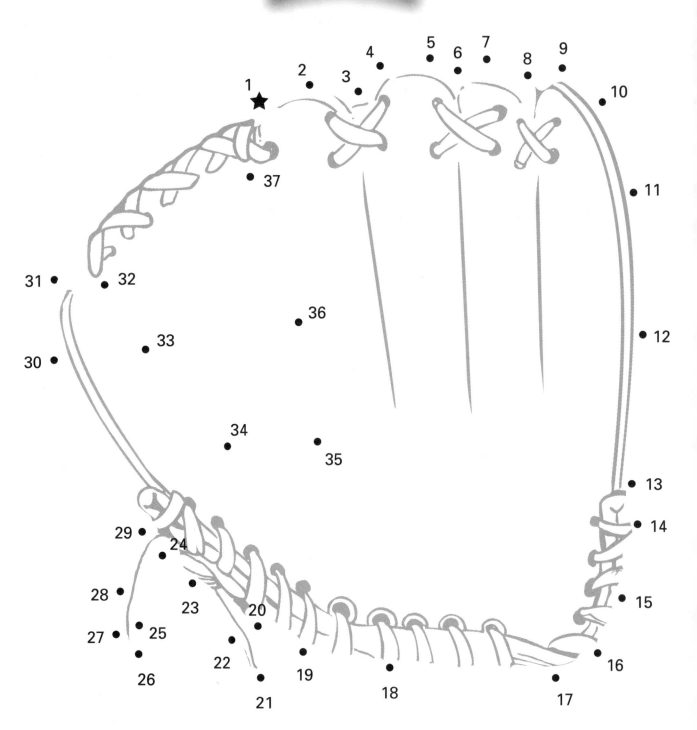

I HAD A GREAT DAY AT **KAUFFMAN STADIUM**

by _____
(your name)

It was a _____ day in _____.
                (weather word)   (month)

The *Royals* were playing the _____ at
                                        (team name)

Kauffman Stadium. We took a _____ to get
                              (car / train / bus)

to Kansas City. I snacked on some _____
                                        (food)

and _____ while we watched the game.
        (food)

I was so excited to see _____
                              (player name)

play today. He's my favorite player! The *Royals*

_____ the game. The score was ____ to ____.
(won / lost)   (score)   (score)

Baseball is my favorite sport, but I also like to

watch _____. I can't wait to come back to
          (sport)

Kauffman Stadium!

A HOME RUN FOR THE Kansas City *Royals*!

SCRAMBLE

Unscramble the letters of these baseball words.

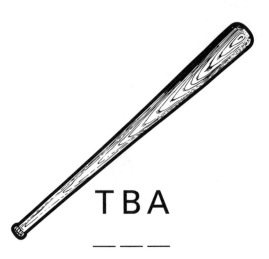

TBA

_ _ _

APC

_ _ _

PMRIEU

_ _ _ _ _ _

SYERJE

_ _ _ _ _ _

VOEGL

_ _ _ _ _

EBAS

_ _ _ _

24   **Solution is on page 54.**

The outfielder is about to make a catch!
Which batter will be out?

Solution is on page 54.

S _ _ _ _ _ _

_ _ _ _ _ _

_ _ _ _ _ _ _

KEY

= C	= R	= V
= E	= I	= S
= G	= N	= T
= H		

26

WORD SEARCH

```
T T P L A Y O F F S D
E W U T H I D E N N N
O S E P F G C O S A B
B E O N W Y I R C S A
F R L U A P A I J G L
T I M D M T R U Q B L
H E V A S E I Y W F P
D S H L M F B O L X A
Y C L A A R Z U N W R
C A F L E Y X Q Q A K
V S S D E R O Z O U L
```

ALL STARS	CHAMPIONS	PLAYOFFS
AMERICAN	DERBY	SERIES
BALLPARK	NATIONAL	TROPHY

Solution is on page 55.

HIDDEN PICTURE

Use the key to color the shapes below and reveal the hidden picture.

KEY

A = Brown **B = Blue** **C = Purple** **D = Green** **E = Yellow** **F = Black**

HINT!
Color inside the lines

T _ _ _ _ _

'

!

KEY

= A	= H	= N	= S	= Y
= D	= I	= O	= T	
= E	= K	= R	= U	

Solution is on page 56.

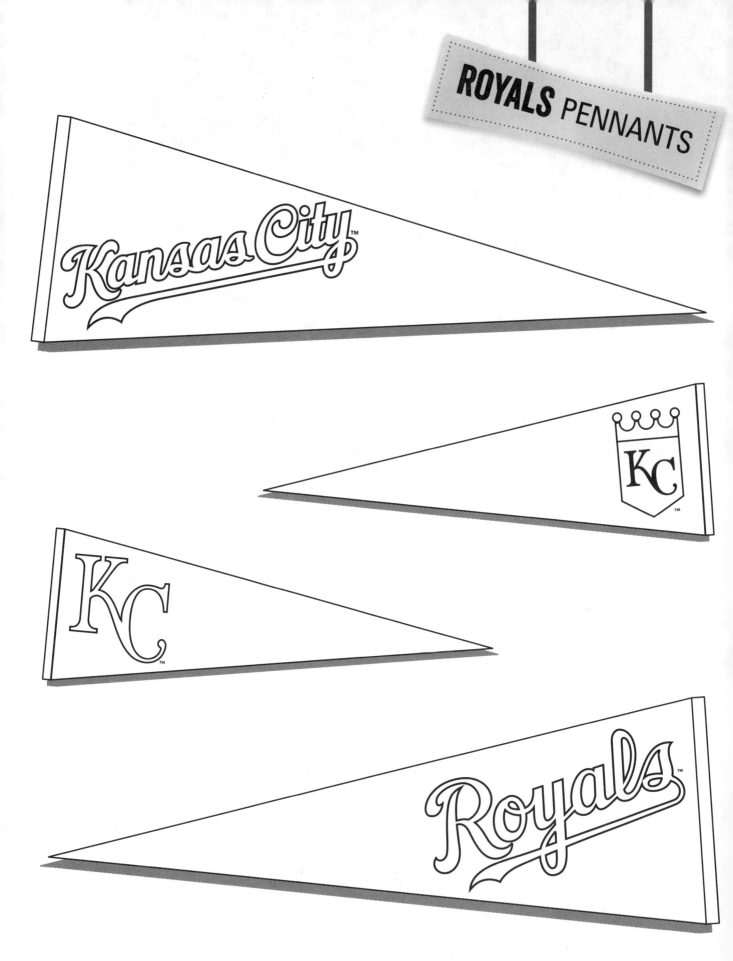

WHAT'S IN A NAME?

How many words can you make using letters found in the three words below?

KANSAS CITY ROYALS

Example: SKY   TALK

1 _____   11 _____

2 _____   12 _____

3 _____   13 _____

4 _____   14 _____

5 _____   15 _____

6 _____   16 _____

7 _____   17 _____

8 _____   18 _____

9 _____   19 _____

10 _____   20 _____

Solution is on page 56.

MY BASEBALL CARD

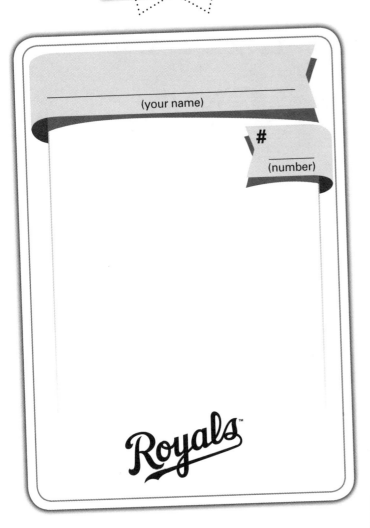

_____ (your name)

_____ (number)

Royals™

Age: _____

Position: _____

Height: _____

Weight: _____

Circle one!

I bat (righty / lefty)
I throw (righty / lefty)

_____ has shown excellent
(your name)
sportsmanship this year!

32

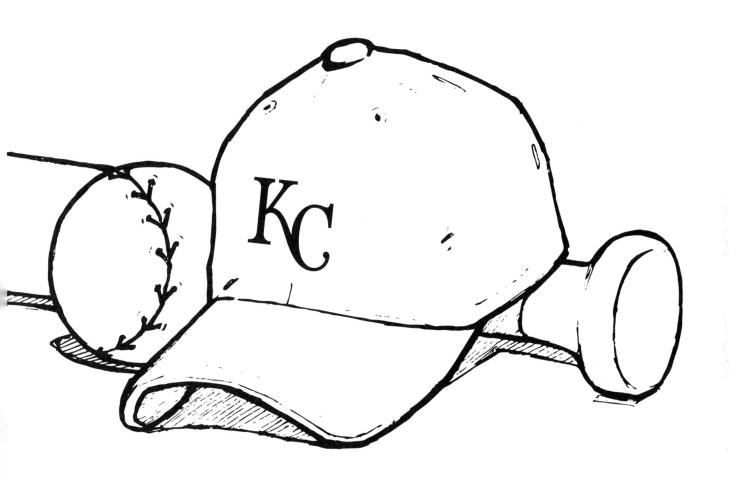

WHAT'S THE SCORE?

Add the runs to find out which team won the game.

Example:	1	2	3	4	5	6	7	8	9	R
INDIANS	0	1	0	0	2	0	0	0	0	3
ROYALS	0	0	1	0	0	1	0	0	2	4

Game 1:	1	2	3	4	5	6	7	8	9	R
INDIANS	0	0	0	0	1	0	2	0	0	
ROYALS	0	2	0	0	1	0	1	1	0	

Game 2:	1	2	3	4	5	6	7	8	9	R
TWINS	0	0	1	0	0	0	0	0	1	
ROYALS	0	3	0	0	2	0	0	2	0	

Game 3:	1	2	3	4	5	6	7	8	9	R
TIGERS	0	3	1	2	0	1	0	1	0	
ROYALS	0	1	0	1	2	0	1	0	1	

Game 4:	1	2	3	4	5	6	7	8	9	R
WHITE SOX	1	1	1	0	1	0	3	0	0	
ROYALS	0	4	1	0	1	1	0	0	2	

34   **Solution is on page 57.**

START HERE

LET'S DRAW!
Use the grid to draw the *MLB*™ logo.

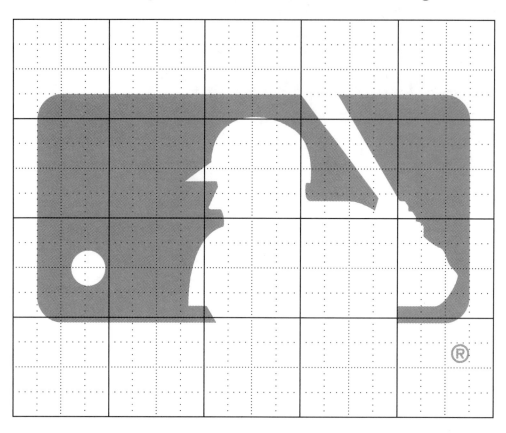

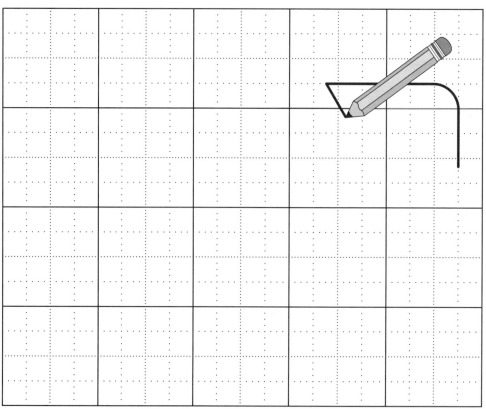

WORD SEARCH

```
B R E T T O T I S R F
N M H B S S I M A U U
D G O D B L S N B Y S
X V W N W H I T E E M
H V S I T V Z L R I A
Z E E H L G N B H T Y
L Q R D F S O X A Q B
Y L F Z A E O M G K E
O Q C U O I H N E A R
X T Y T O G O A N R R
J J Q E F Z K A E J Y
```

BRETT	MAYBERRY	SABERHAGEN
HERZOG	MONTGOMERY	WHITE
HOWSER	OTIS	WILSON

Solution is on page 58.

ONE LUCKY Kansas City Royals FAN

T A K E M E

O U T T O T H E

B A L L G A M E

KEY

= A	= G	= L	= T
= B	= H	= M	= U
= E	= K	= O	

FIND THE DIFFERENCES

Can you find all **four** differences between the two images below?

40   **Solution is on page 59.**

SCRAMBLE

Unscramble the letters of these baseball positions.

I T C H R E P

P I T C H E R

C A H T E R C

_ _ _ _ _ _ _

R I F T S

_ _ _ _ _

SABMANE

_ _ _ _ _ _ _

T U O L I E F D R E

_ _ _ _ _ _ _ _ _

E R T T A B

_ _ _ _ _ _

Solution is on page 59.

WHAT'S IN A NAME?

How many words can you make using letters
found in the three words below?

MAJOR LEAGUE BASEBALL

Example: AREA   BEAR

1 _____   11 _____

2 _____   12 _____

3 _____   13 _____

4 _____   14 _____

5 _____   15 _____

6 _____   16 _____

7 _____   17 _____

8 _____   18 _____

9 _____   19 _____

10 _____   20 _____

          Solution is on page 60.

IS THE BATTER SAFE?
Follow the maze to find out!

OUT!

SAFE!

START HERE

Solution is on page 60.

CROSSWORD PUZZLE
Use your knowledge of the *Royals* to solve the puzzle.

Across

4. The *Royals* played against the _____ in the 2014 *World Series*.

5. A golden _____ sits above the giant screen in center field at *Kauffman Stadium*.

7. The controversial "Pine Tar Incident" occurred in a game that took place between the *Royals* and the _____ on July 24, 1983.

8. Retired *Royals* second baseman Frank _____ won eight *American League* defensive awards during his career.

Down

1. Manager Dick _____ led the *Royals* to three division titles and one *World Series* Championship.

2. On October 27, 1985, the *Royals* defeated the _____ to win their first *World Series* Championship.

3. "The K" is a nickname for _____ *Stadium*.

6. Number 5 was retired by the *Royals* in honor of famous third baseman George _____.

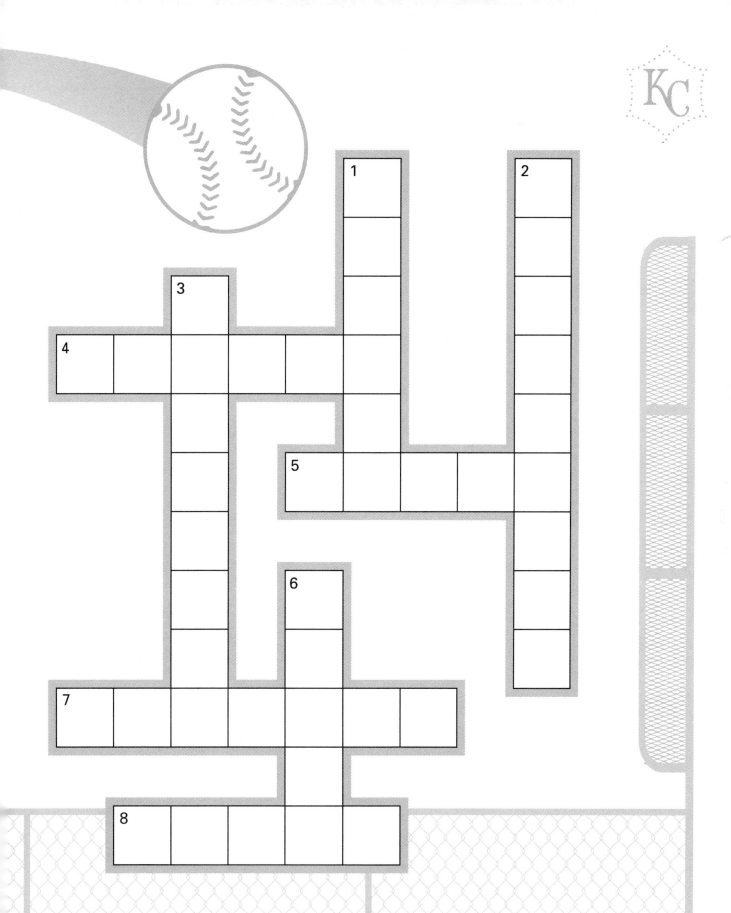

HIDDEN PICTURE

Use the key to color the shapes below and reveal the hidden picture.

KEY

A = Dark Blue   **B = Light Blue**   **C = Light Gray**   **D = Dark Gray (or black)**   **E = Tan**

HINT!
Color inside the lines

WORD SEARCH

```
C T J I Q U E K R R W
P A I U D L Z K T L V
E M T G P U H C U P B
N Z S C M B G O A T A
U P Y T H L F O K P S
C C D U R E Y B U I E
F V W U R I R S I T B
O W K I O V K E R C A
Q X P G L O V E Q H L
E M Z D R G Z X T E L
U Z S O G S M T N R Q
```

BASEBALL	DUGOUT	PITCHER
CAP	FOUL	STRIKE
CATCHER	GLOVE	UMPIRE

Solution is on page 61.

WHICH *Kansas City Royals* MASCOT IMAGE IS DIFFERENT FROM THE REST?

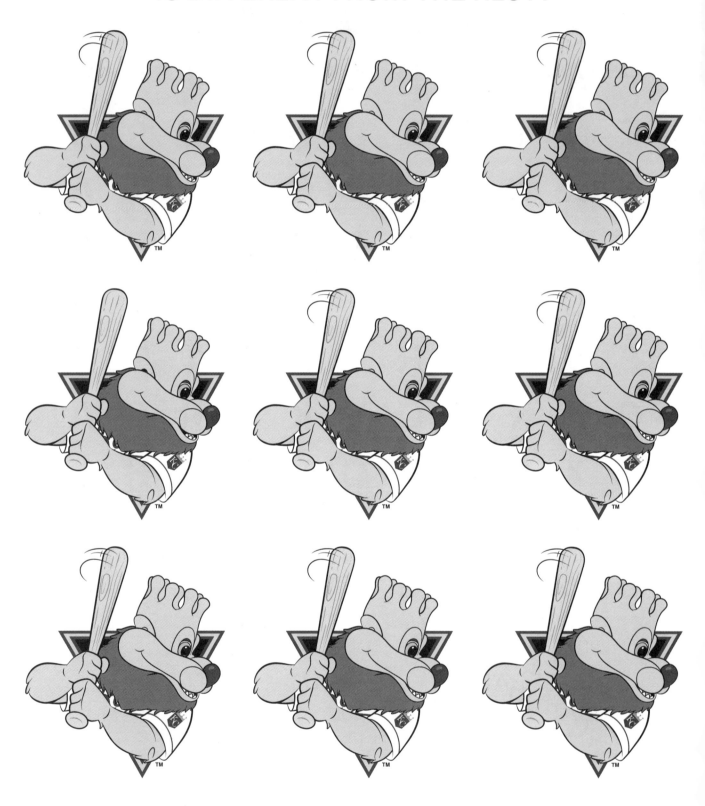

Solution is on page 62.

SOLUTIONS

Page 2

Page 3

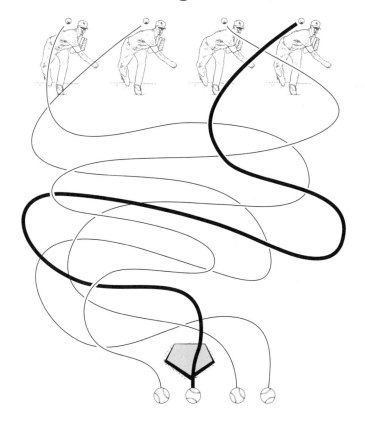

Page 5

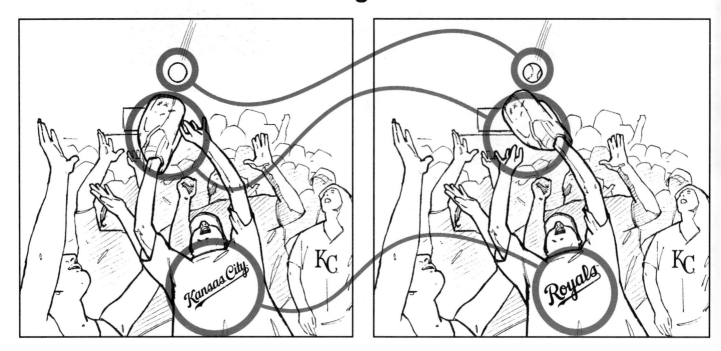

Page 6

Page 7

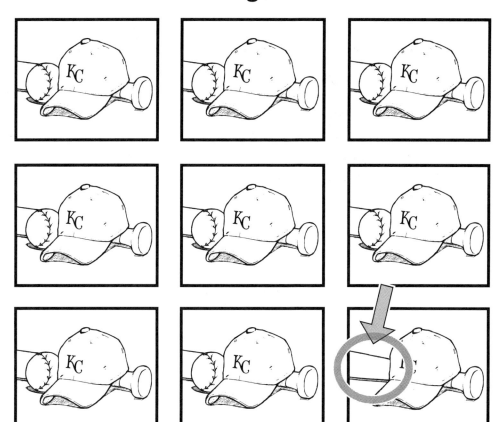

Page 9

FOREVER

ROYAL

Page 10

6 1st base

3 2nd base

5 3rd base

9 batter's box

11 catcher's box

7 coach's box

2 foul line

12 home plate

4 infield

10 on-deck circle

1 outfield

8 pitcher's mound

Page 12

SODA

HOT DOG

POPCORN

PRETZEL

ICE CREAM

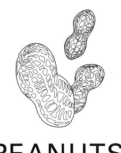

PEANUTS

Page 16

Page 19

Page 24

BAT

CAP

UMPIRE

JERSEY

GLOVE

BASE

Page 25

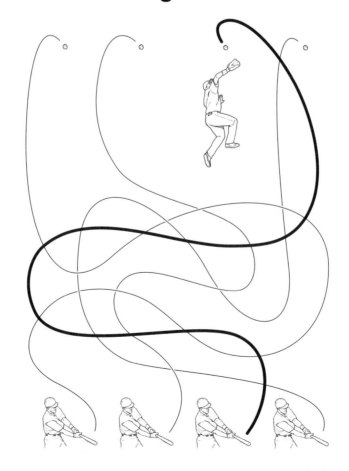

Page 26

S E V E N T H

I N N I N G

S T R E T C H

Page 27

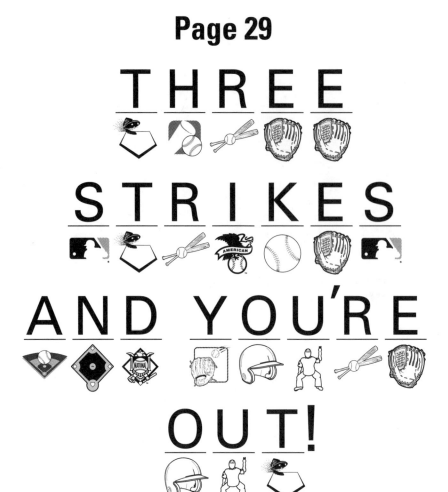

T H R E E
S T R I K E S
A N D Y O U ' R E
O U T !

Page 31

Below are just a few examples of words that could be made with these letters.

K A N S A S C I T Y R O Y A L S

across	crayons	lost	sassy	sly	star	task
act	cry	nail	sat	snack	stay	tiara
ant	crystal	noisy	satin	snort	sticky	tin
art	ink	oat	say	snot	stir	track
carton	knit	oil	scar	soar	stock	trail
cat	last	ratio	scary	sock	stork	trick
clay	liar	ray	scorn	sonic	story	tricky
coat	lion	rock	sit	stain	strain	try
corn	loan	salsa	skirt	stairs	tail	yarn

Page 34

Game 1:	1	2	3	4	5	6	7	8	9	R
INDIANS	0	0	0	0	1	0	2	0	0	3
ROYALS	0	2	0	0	1	0	1	1	0	5

Game 2:	1	2	3	4	5	6	7	8	9	R
TWINS	0	0	1	0	0	0	0	0	1	2
ROYALS	0	3	0	0	2	0	0	2	0	7

Game 3:	1	2	3	4	5	6	7	8	9	R
TIGERS	0	3	1	2	0	1	0	1	0	8
ROYALS	0	1	0	1	2	0	1	0	1	6

Game 4:	1	2	3	4	5	6	7	8	9	R
WHITE SOX	1	1	1	0	1	0	3	0	0	7
ROYALS	0	4	1	0	1	1	0	0	2	9

Page 35

Page 37

```
B R E T T O T I S R F
N M H B S S I M A U U
D G O D B L S N B Y S
X V W N W H I T E E M
H V S I T V Z L R I A
Z E E H L G N B H T Y
L Q R D F S O X A Q B
Y L F Z A E O M G K E
O Q C U O I H N E A R
X T Y T O G O A N R R
J J Q E F Z K A E J Y
```

Page 39

TAKE ME

OUT TO THE

BALLGAME

Page 40

Page 41

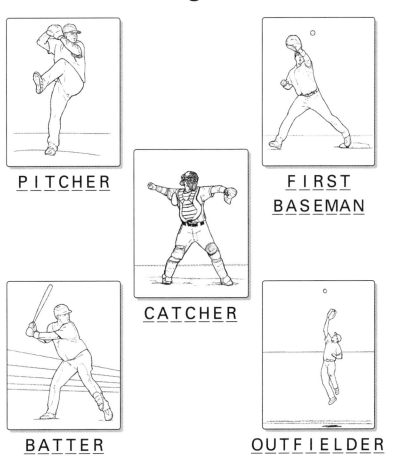

PITCHER

FIRST
BASEMAN

CATCHER

BATTER

OUTFIELDER

Page 42

Below are just a few examples of words that could be made with these letters.

<u>M A J O R   L E A G U E   B A S E B A L L</u>

ajar	beam	bull	gore	meal	reel	seem
alas	bear	ease	lamb	mole	roll	sell
also	bell	else	lame	mule	rule	slab
area	blob	game	lobe	muse	saga	slam
aura	blue	gear	lube	ogre	sage	soar
ball	blur	germ	lure	oral	sale	some
barb	boar	glee	male	rage	seal	sour
bare	bomb	glue	mall	real	seam	urge
base	bulb	goal	mars	ream	sear	user

Page 43

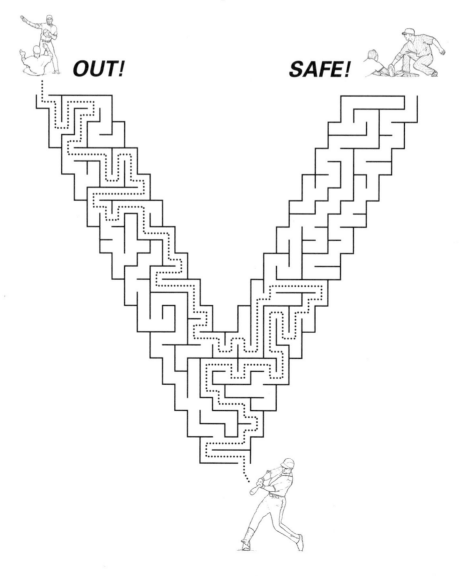

OUT!   SAFE!

Page 45

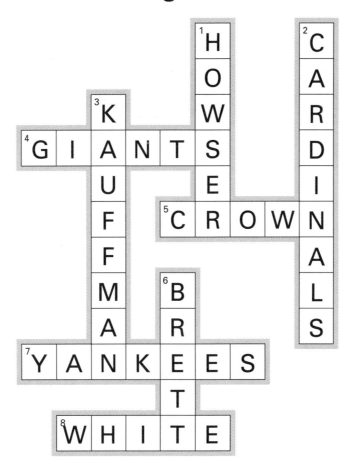

Page 47

Page 48

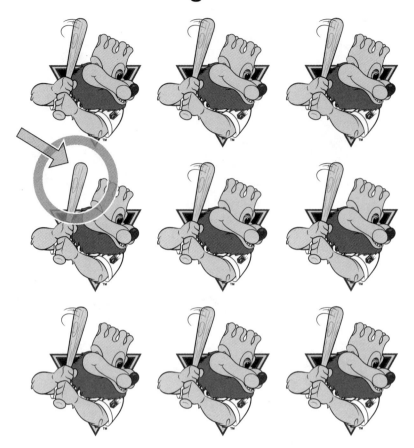